EDGE
BOOKS™

THE SCIENCE BEHIND
NATURAL PHENOMENA

THE SCIENCE BEHIND

WONDERS OF THE
SKY

AURORAS, MOONBOWS, AND ST. ELMO'S FIRE

BY ALLAN MOREY

CONSULTANT:
DR. SANDRA MATHER
PROFESSOR EMERITA, DEPARTMENT OF GEOLOGY AND ASTRONOMY,
WEST CHESTER UNIVERSITY, WEST CHESTER, PENNSYLVANIA

*A corona discharge can be seen
on this overhead power cable.*

CAPSTONE PRESS
a capstone imprint

Edge Books are published by Capstone Press, 1710 Roe Crest Drive, North Mankato, Minnesota 56003
www.mycapstone.com

Library of Congress Cataloging-in-Publication Data
Names: Morey, Allan, author.
Title: The science behind wonders of the sky : Aurora borealis, moonbows, and St. Elmo's fire / by Allan Morey.
Description: North Mankato, Minnesota : Capstone Press, [2017] | Series: Edge books. The science behind natural phenomena | Audience: Ages 9–15. | Audience: Grades 4 to 6. | Includes bibliographical references and index.
Identifiers: LCCN 2016005755 | ISBN 9781515707776 (library binding) | ISBN 9781515707820 (paperback) | ISBN 9781515707875 (ebook pdf)
Subjects: LCSH: Atmospheric physics—Juvenile literature. | Sky—Juvenile literature. | Earth (Planet)—Miscellanea—Juvenile literature.
Classification: LCC QC863.5 .M667 2017 | DDC 551.55—dc23
LC record available at http://lccn.loc.gov/2016005755

Editorial Credits
Linda Staniford, editor; Terri Poburka, designer;
Svetlana Zhurkin, media researcher; Katy LaVigne, production specialist

Photo Credits
NASA: Bill Ingalls, 5; Newscom: Photoshot/Bruce Coleman/Kim Taylor, 15, Xinhua News Agency/Tourism Ministry, 26, ZUMA Press/National News, 27; North Wind Picture Archives, 28; Shutterstock: amelissimo, 4, Andrea J. Smith, 20–21, ArtMari, 18, Bridget Calip, 19 (bottom), C_Eng-Wong Photography, 19 (top left), Daniel Schreiber, 8, daulon, 7, Designua, 23 (inset), 24, Elenarts, 13 (right), fabiodevilla, 17, Georgios Kollidas, 15 (bottom), Glamorous Images, 19 (top right), Juhku, 23, lfstewart, 21 (middle), Muskoka Stock Photos, 11, Peter Hermes Furian, 10, Pi-Lens, 19 (nimbostratus), Pitsanu Kraichana, 19 (middle left), Shin Okamoto, cover, Shooarts, 12–13, Stefano Garau, 19 (cumulonimbus), 25, traskevych, 19 (middle right), Vadim Sadovski, 17 (middle), VikaSuh, 1 and throughout; Wikimedia: Nitromethane, 29

Printed and bound in China.
007720

TABLE OF CONTENTS

OUR GREAT BIG SKY

Look up at the sky. It is more than just a dome of air. Even on a clear day, a lot is going on there. Winds swirl about. Water vapor rises and condenses into clouds. Sunlight shines down to warm our planet, and specks of space dust burn up in the **atmosphere.**

No wonder people have been awestruck by the heavens. Wondrous and frightening things happen up in the sky. Ancient people did not understand what caused these events. They believed gods caused the blowing winds and crackling lightning. People saw the sky gods as the most powerful, feared, and respected of all the gods.

Sights such as auroras and **meteor** showers still amaze us today. But now, science helps us understand what causes these incredible natural **phenomena.**

Zeus

Mythological Sky Gods

HORUS—Egyptian

JUPITER—Roman

TYR—Norse

ZEUS—Greek

A meteor streaks across the sky during the annual Perseid meteor shower. →

atmosphere—the layer of gases surrounding a planet

meteor—a piece of rock or dust that enters Earth's atmosphere, causing a streak of light in the sky

phenomena—very unusual or remarkable events

AURORAS

Auroras are one of nature's most spectacular shows. On dark winter nights when there is no moonlight, they appear as colored ribbons of light across the sky. Green is the most common color, but rare displays of deep red, curtains of blue, and streams of purple have also been seen.

Auroras are caused by the Sun. The surface of the Sun is an extremely violent place. **Plasma** heaves and roils. Eruptions eject loops of hot gases, called prominences, into space. Solar flares burst across its surface.

As the Sun rotates, its intense activity flings tiny bits of matter into space. These particles have an electrical charge. As they speed away from the Sun, they create solar winds.

Around Earth is a magnetic field, a flow of energy that moves from the North Pole to the South Pole. The magnetic field protects our planet from the charged particles streaming from the Sun. Most of them simply bounce off the magnetic field. But where it is weakest, at the poles, these particles can reach Earth's upper atmosphere.

Earth's magnetic field protects our planet from solar winds. ⟶

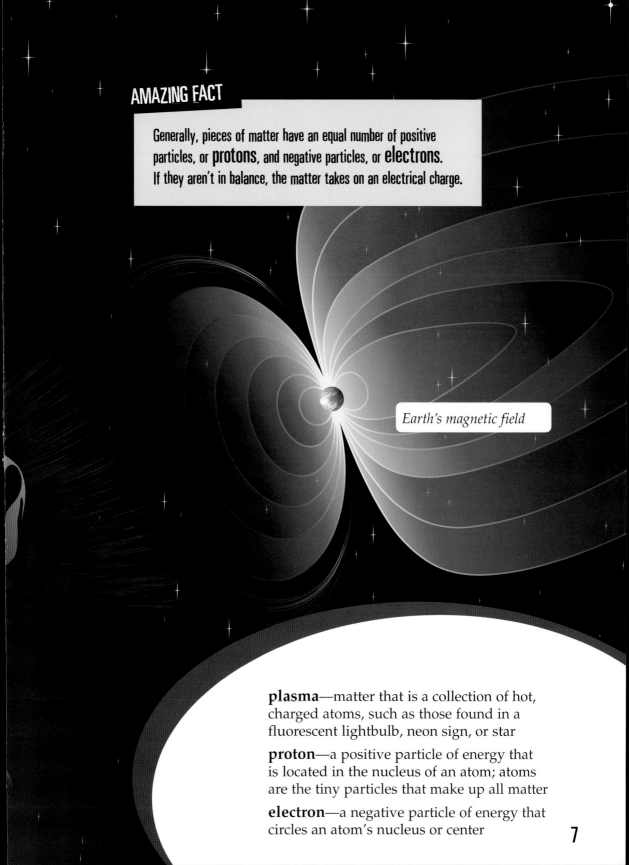

Generally, pieces of matter have an equal number of positive particles, or **protons**, and negative particles, or **electrons**. If they aren't in balance, the matter takes on an electrical charge.

Earth's magnetic field

plasma—matter that is a collection of hot, charged atoms, such as those found in a fluorescent lightbulb, neon sign, or star

proton—a positive particle of energy that is located in the nucleus of an atom; atoms are the tiny particles that make up all matter

electron—a negative particle of energy that circles an atom's nucleus or center

When charged particles hit Earth's atmosphere, they react with the gases far up in the atmosphere. Different gases make different colored auroras. A reaction with oxygen makes the auroras green and red. A reaction with nitrogen makes them blue and purple.

Some of the best places to see auroras are in the far north, around the Arctic Circle. The aurora borealis, also called the northern lights, appears over Canada and Greenland. It can be seen from Scandinavia to Siberia. On rare occasions it can be seen farther south, in the northern United States and even in northern parts of the United Kingdom.

Aurora Legends

To people living hundreds of years ago, the aurora borealis was both frightening and awe-inspiring. It became the source of many legends. Some people believed the lights were evil spirits or omens of disaster and disease. In Greenland people thought they were spirits of dead children. In Scotland they were said to be warring spirits.

Others had a kinder view of these colorful lights. The Inuit people of Alaska believed they were animal spirits dancing in the sky. The Algonquin Indians, of eastern Canada, thought the northern lights were fires lit by Nanahbozho, the creator. According to myths, Nanahbozho built these fires so his people would know he was thinking of them.

South of the equator, these lights are called the aurora australis, or southern lights. They are mirror-images of the northern lights and appear at the same time. But they are rarely seen. Few people live far enough south to spot them.

Antarctica is the best place to see the southern lights. They also appear over the southern tip of Chile and southern parts of New Zealand. Sometimes people see them in southern Australia and South Africa.

MOONBOWS

Everyone has seen a rainbow arcing across the sky. These colorful effects are created by sunlight and water droplets floating in the air. But have you ever heard of a moonbow? Moonbows and rainbows are created in much the same way. Moonbows just happen at night.

Light travels in waves, somewhat like water in the ocean. But light waves are too tiny to see. Each color of light has a slightly different wavelength. Violet is the shortest, and red the longest. Sunlight is made up of many colors. Usually, we cannot see the separate colors because they all move together.

That changes when sunlight hits a water droplet. The light bends, or **refracts**, as it moves from the air into the water. Because of their different wavelengths, colors don't bend the same. Violet bends the most, and red bends the least. Sunlight's colors separate when they refract. Then we see a rainbow.

This also happens at night, as sunlight reflects off the Moon and travels to Earth. Moonbows arc across the sky like a rainbow. Sometimes they are seen far up in the clouds, in a circle around the moon. Moonbows also form over waterfalls. As water splashes down from great heights, water droplets rise into the air and catch the moonlight.

When light passes through a prism it splits into different colors. Each color bends differently. Water droplets have the same effect, which is why we see rainbows and moonbows.

A "bow" can occur anytime sunlight travels through water droplets. So there are also fogbows and dewbows. The dew can be on a spider's web or the grass in your front yard.

refract—to bend light as it passes through a substance at an angle, such as light passing through a water droplet

COMETS

Mercury Venus Earth Mars Asteroid Belt Jupiter Saturn Uranus Neptune

Comets come from regions at the edge of our solar system.

Many objects **orbit** the Sun. Some are huge like the planets. Others are just specks of dust. But none zoom through our solar system more dramatically than comets.

Comets travel at incredible speeds, upwards of 100,000 miles (160,000 kilometers) per hour. Their long, **elliptical** orbits take them from the outer edges of our solar system to near collisions with our Sun.

orbit—the path an object follows as it goes around the Sun or a planet

elliptical—shaped like an oval

asteroid—a chunk of rock too small to be called a planet that orbits the Sun; most asteroids are found between the orbits of Mars and Jupiter

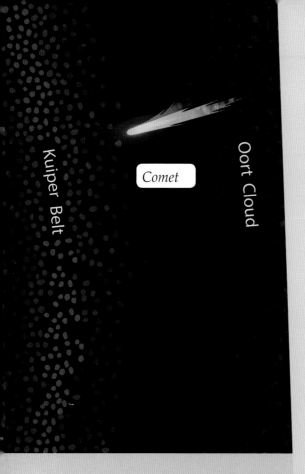

Kuiper Belt

Comet

Oort Cloud

The Rosetta Mission

The European Space Agency (ESA) launched the Rosetta Mission in 2004. This spacecraft landed a probe on Comet 67P/Churyumov-Gerasimenko. The probe sent back to Earth information about what the comet is made of and what its surface is like.

There are two types of comets. Kuiper Belt comets come from just beyond Neptune's orbit. The dwarf planets, Pluto and Eris, are found in this **asteroid** belt. Some Kuiper Belt comets take a few years to complete an orbit. Others take several hundred years. Comet 67P/Churyumov–Gerasimenko takes 6½ years to complete one orbit through the solar system.

Beyond the Kuiper Belt, in the outermost reaches of our solar system, is the Oort Cloud. It is mostly made up of ice and dust and is the home of long-term comets. These comets take thousands or even millions of years to circle the Sun.

Most comets are only a few miles in diameter. They are too small and too far away for us to see most of the time. But as they come near to the Sun, things change dramatically.

Comets are made mostly of ice and frozen gases and are covered in space dust. Scientists refer to them as "dirty snowballs." When a comet nears the Sun, the ice and frozen gases start to melt. As they melt, they form a thin atmosphere, called a coma, around the comet.

Remember those charged particles that help create the aurora borealis? Streams of these charged particles, called solar winds, sweep over the comet. They push a comet's coma and dust out into space, creating the comet's tail.

As the comet gets closer to the Sun, its tail grows longer. Sunlight reflects off the particles in the comet's tail, making it a spectacular sight in the night sky.

Edmond Halley (1656–1742) was an English astronomer who studied historic reports of comets. In his book *Astronomiae Cometicae Synopsis,* he came to the conclusion that comets seen in 1531, 1607, and 1682 were actually the same comet.

At the time, people didn't realize that comets orbited the Sun. Halley died before his predicted return of the comet in 1758, but now it is named after him.

Halley's Comet passes by Earth about every 75 years. It was last seen in 1986, and it is predicted to return in 2061.

METEOROIDS, METEORS, AND METEOR SHOWERS

Have you ever seen a "falling star" streaking across the sky and made a wish? Well, it wasn't actually a star. Stars are huge, many times larger than Earth, although they look tiny because they are so far away from us. The Sun that Earth rotates around is a star. But "falling stars" are small rocks called asteroids burning up in Earth's atmosphere.

Billions of asteroids float out in space. Some are hundreds of miles across. But most are much smaller, ranging from pebble-sized rocks to specks of dust left behind by comets. These small asteroids are called meteoroids.

As a meteoroid enters Earth's atmosphere, gas particles bombard it and create friction. The friction heats the meteoroid and breaks it apart. Then a brilliant light streaks across the sky. We call this phenomenon a meteor.

AMAZING FACT

Most meteoroids burn up in Earth's atmosphere, but if part of one reaches Earth's surface, it is called a meteorite.

Meteor showers occur when Earth passes through the debris of a comet's tail. Sand-sized specs of matter enter Earth's atmosphere and burn up. As they burn, they light up the night sky like fireworks.

The Leonid meteor shower occurs yearly, about mid-November. It is seen when Earth passes through the debris left by the comet Tempel-Tuttle. Hundreds of meteors can be seen at night during this shower.

CLOUD FORMATIONS

Clouds are an important part of the water cycle. The Sun heats the surface of oceans, lakes, and rivers. The warm water evaporates and turns into water vapor, a gaseous form. Water vapor rises into the atmosphere because of convection. Hotter, less dense matter moves above cooler, denser matter. Water vapor is warmer and lighter than the air around it, so it rises.

High in the atmosphere, the water vapor cools and condenses. It grows into tiny water droplets. The water droplets are visible as clouds and fog. When the water droplets grow large enough, they fall as rain or snow.

All clouds form from the same material: water. But the surprising thing is that they can come in a variety of shapes and sizes, and even colors.

This diagram shows the water cycle.

cirrus

stratus

cumulus

nimbus

Basic Cloud Types

CIRRUS—thin, wispy-looking clouds made of ice crystals that form high up in the atmosphere

CUMULUS—dense clouds with white, fluffy tops

STRATUS—thin, gray, sheet-like clouds stretching across the sky

NIMBUS—tall, dark clouds, often like huge puffs of smoke, that bring heavy rain or snow

These basic cloud types can be combined to form new cloud types:

CUMULONIMBUS—towering thunderstorm clouds

NIMBOSTRATUS—gray clouds that produce a light rain or snow

CIRROSTRATUS—thin, white clouds

cumulonimbus

nimbostratus

cirrostratus

Along with the standard clouds, some extremely odd formations can form in the atmosphere. Asperitas clouds are among the most dramatic. Unlike most other clouds, they do not have a flat bottom. Sometimes asperitas clouds appear as deep waves stretching across the sky. Other times they make the sky look like an upside down ocean on a stormy day.

Asperitas clouds are an amazing sight. They have been seen in the United States, from the Great Plains to the southeastern states. They have also been spotted over parts of northern Europe.

Asperitas clouds often appear when there are strong winds following a thunderstorm.

Asperitas clouds are low clouds, hanging less than 6,000 feet (1,800 meters) in the air. Scientists do not fully understand how they form. They think asperitas clouds might be connected to storm clouds. They are most often seen after a thunderstorm has passed, though they do not produce rain. One thought is that the rough winds at the tail end of a storm create these wavy clouds.

Lenticular Clouds

Lenticular clouds are another strange cloud formation. They usually occur above a mountain range or other high object. If it is cold enough, the moisture in the air blowing over the mountain condenses to form a disc-shaped cloud. People have mistaken these clouds for UFOs because of their shape.

Perhaps some of the most amazing cloud formations are night clouds, or noctilucent clouds. They are most often seen in cold, polar regions, and they occur way up in the mesospheric layer of the atmosphere. Another name for them is polar mesospheric clouds.

Typically air gets cooler as it rises in the atmosphere. The drop in temperature causes water vapor to condense into water droplets. But in the mesospheric layer, those water droplets freeze. Noctilucent clouds form from ice crystals and specks of dust high in the atmosphere.

Noctilucent clouds are seen after sunset. When the Sun dips below the **horizon**, sunlight shines up at these clouds. Sunlight illuminates the clouds because of their altitude. They glow blue-white in the night sky.

Incipient clouds are a more dramatic type of noctilucent cloud. The difference is the color. Sunlight refracts through ice crystals in the clouds. The colors separate, much like how they do to create a rainbow. These clouds glow with all colors of the rainbow.

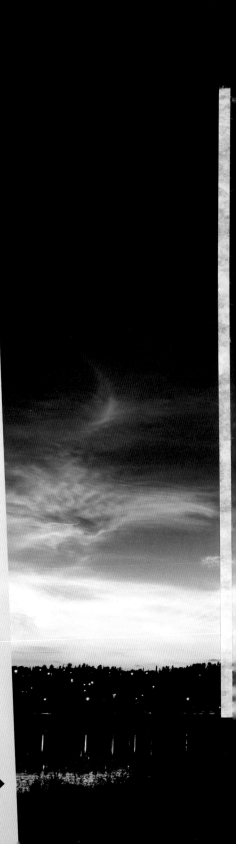

Noctilucent clouds appear on summer nights. They often have formations such as whirls, knots, and bands.

Layers of the Atmosphere

The atmosphere is divided into several layers:

THERMOSPHERE—56 miles (90 km)
   where auroras occur

MESOSPHERE—31–53 miles (50-85 km)
   where most meteoroids burn up

STRATOSPHERE—7–30 miles (11–48 km)
   where the ozone layer occurs

TROPOSPHERE—7 miles (11 km)
   where most clouds form

horizon—the line where the sky
and the land or sea seem to meet

23

THUNDER AND LIGHTNING

Flashes of lightning are one of the most common phenomena to light up the sky. As we know, a booming clap of thunder accompanies every lightning bolt.

These effects start up in the clouds. You might not realize that as they float across the sky, clouds are alive with activity. Water vapor condenses. Winds swirl. Air particles smash into one another. Scientists aren't exactly sure how this happens, but some of those particles become electrically charged.

During a thunderstorm, particles with a negative charge collect at the bottom of a cloud. At the same time, positively charged particles gather near the ground, including treetops and other tall objects. When the difference in the charges gets to a certain point—ZAP! There is a discharge of electricity called lightning. Lightning neutralizes the difference between the charges.

Lightning creates heat as it moves through the air. Heat causes molecules to expand. Thunder is the sound of rapidly expanding air molecules.

Lightning is formed when particles with opposite charges attract each other.

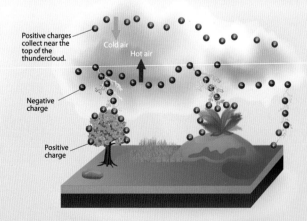

Positive charges collect near the top of the thundercloud.

Cold air

Hot air

Negative charge

Positive charge

We see lightning before hearing thunder. That is because light travels faster than sound. Light travels at 186,282 miles (299,792 km) per second. Sound travels at 1,087 feet (331 m) per second. It takes approximately 5 seconds for the sound of thunder to travel 1 mile (1.6 km).

Sheet lightning is reflected by clouds and can light up the whole sky.

Types of Lightning

There are many different types of lightning. Here are some of them:

FORKED LIGHTNING—jagged lines of light with branches that can jump between clouds or from a cloud to the ground

SHEET LIGHTNING—flashes that light up whole clouds

ANVIL LIGHTNING—lightning that can strike a long distance from the thunderstorm, where the sky is cloudless. It is sometimes called a "bolt from the blue."

BALL LIGHTNING—a rare type of lightning that is round like a ball and often hisses. Ball lightning can pass through windows. It may last a few minutes and can explode with a loud bang.

SPRITES AND JETS—differently shaped bursts of lightning that can occur above storm clouds

When lightning is part of a volcanic eruption, you see something that is truly amazing. Volcanic lightning looks like it could be a special effect in a science fiction movie.

Volcanoes are one of nature's most destructive forces. They occur when pressure builds up deep within Earth. Magma, or molten rock, is then pushed up through cracks in Earth's crust. Volcanic eruptions spew lava, rocks, clouds of gases, and tons of ash into the sky. Plumes of volcanic ash can block out the Sun, disrupt air travel, and cause temperatures to drop a few degrees.

Atmospheric conditions cause frequent thunderstorms over the Catatumbo River.

AMAZING FACT

Almost every day, a thunderstorm forms over the mouth of the Catatumbo River in Venezuela. The frequent lightning strikes caused by this storm have been nicknamed Catatumbo lightning.

Lightning strikes around an erupting volcano in Japan.

A lot is going on in a normal cloud. But imagine the activity happening in a cloud being shot into the sky by a volcano! Positively and negatively charged particles form in the ash cloud. Just like with other types of lightning, the particles collect until—CRACK!

The **turbulence** in a volcanic cloud pushes this reaction to the extreme. Many streaks of lightning crack through an ash cloud. They can be miles long.

turbulence—the violent movement of air or water

ST. ELMO'S FIRE

Have you ever seen a glowing light on the top of a lamppost or antenna? In the past, sailors noticed this light atop their ships' masts. They dubbed it St. Elmo's Fire, after the patron saint of sailors. Sailors usually saw the light at the end of a storm, so they thought it meant the saint was watching over them.

What they really saw was a corona discharge. After a storm, the air between the clouds and the ground is filled with energy. As the energy gathers around tall metal objects, gas molecules in the air start to lose electrons. The positively charged gas molecules then form glowing plasma. A sizzling sound is often heard with the eerie light.

St. Elmo's Fire is just one of the incredible and strange phenomena that can be seen in the sky. Science helps us understand many of these events, but some still baffle us. Others have yet to be discovered. Finding out about the science behind these natural wonders helps us appreciate the amazing world in which we live.

A corona discharge can be seen on this overhead power cable.

Glossary

asteroid (AS-tuh-royd)—a chunk of rock too small to be called a planet that orbits the Sun; most asteroids are found between the orbits of Mars and Jupiter

atmosphere (AT-muhss-fihr)—the layer of gases surrounding a planet; Earth's atmosphere is made up mostly of nitrogen and oxygen.

electron (i-LEK-tron)—a negative particle of energy that circles an atom's nucleus or center

elliptical (ell-IP-ti-kal)—shaped like an oval

horizon (huh-RYE-zuhn)—the line where the sky and the land or sea seem to meet

meteor (MEE-tee-ur)—a piece of rock or dust that enters Earth's atmosphere causing a streak of light in the sky

orbit (OR-bit)—the path an object follows as it goes around the Sun or a planet

phenomena (fe-NOM-eh-nuh)—very unusual or remarkable events

plasma (PLAZ-muh)—matter that is a collection of hot, charged atoms, such as those found in a fluorescent lightbulb, neon sign, or star

proton (PRO-tahn)—a positive particle of energy that is located in the nucleus of an atom; atoms are the tiny particles that make up all matter

refract (ri-FRACT)—to bend light as it passes through a substance at an angle, such as light passing through a water droplet

turbulence (TUR-byoo-luns)—the violent movement of air or water

Read More

Atkinson, Stuart. *Comets, Asteroids, and Meteors.* Astronaut Travel Guides. Chicago: Raintree, 2013.

Hunter, Nick. *Northern Lights.* The Night Sky: and other amazing sights. Chicago: Capstone Heinemann Library, 2013.

Shea, Therese. *Freaky Weather Stories.* Freaky True Science. New York: Gareth Stevens Publishing, 2016.

Internet Sites

FactHound offers a safe, fun way to find Internet sites related to this book. All of the sites on FactHound have been researched by our staff.

Here's all you do:

Visit *www.facthound.com*

Type in this code: 9781515707776

 Check out projects, games and lots more at **www.capstonekids.com**

Critical Thinking Using the Common Core

1. Why do we see lightning before we hear thunder?
   (Key Ideas and Details)

2. Explain the difference between a meteoroid and a meteorite.
   (Craft and Structure)

3. Why do we see different colors in a moonbow?
   (Key Ideas and Details)

Index